GOD'S PROPHETIC EQUILIBRIUM

The Balance of God's Supernatural Trichotomy

Anita Snowden, D.D.

LOVE CLONES
publishing

Love Clones Publishing
www.lcpublishing.net

Printed in the United States of America

First Printing, 2016

ISBN: 978-0692702567

King James Version Scripture quotations marked "KJV" are taken from the Holy Bible, King James Version (Public Domain).

Publishers:
Love Clones Publishing
Dallas, TX 75205
www.lcpublishing.net

DEDICATION

To my dear husband and best friend, Michael. Sharing this journey with me is a real blessing.

To my beloved children, Nicole, Brian, and Joshua. Thank you for loving Mommy.

FOREWORD

Prophetess Anita Snowden has deep roots in her faith with God. From early childhood, she has been a 'PK', Preacher's Kid, and was occupied in all phases of church activities. It is rewarding to her to see so many hearts and minds leaning on her every word to hear her announce choice phrases which have been placed on her heart for the people of God. Her ministry has reached permeating proportions ranging from plain old fashioned taught ways to contemporaneous one-on-one counseling from a winning testimony to a full church revival. One would have to know Prophetess Snowden's past in order to appreciate where God is taking her now and in her future. She was viewed as ordinary among her peers who had little inclination that God was raising her up to be a mouthpiece for Him. She now stands proficient while preaching God's word to others, issuing out of the bible, warnings and rewards.

Hidden within her title, *God's Prophetic Equilibrium*, is nothing short of a divine revelation to the Body of Christ on the importance of each assignment, operating under the anointing, and advancement in the Kingdom of God. Each of us desires that God will use us in some special way to bless His people and be blessed ourselves. An example would be that of someone who has the gift of healing. This in itself is an admirable gift to operate in, using our God-given gift to release others of pain and suffering. However, what we cannot allow ourselves to do is misuse any gift from God as Balaam did; he used his gift for carnal reasons, lowing the high standards of God for mere pence; being vainly puffed up by his fleshly mind. That is the general trend today; too many persons with God-given gifts are used in mercantilism, for personal gains, without maintain on the needs of God's people.

Prophetess Anita Snowden's book has emerged as a spokesperson for God. Prophetess Snowden wants to extend to you, the reader, special advantages discoverable through her ministry in words, thoughts, and instructions so that you might find balance as you seek to escalate in your work for the Lord.

Please be direct as you contemplate the distinctive insights that'll be found in this precious work, and do more than merely read it to yourself; seek to connect to her transcendence, through divine guidance - prayerfully, meditatively, and spiritually. In doing so, I pray that God will give you the particulars you so earnestly desire to "finish your course." Please hear the wisdom of this book and use this book to the glory of God, and God will reward you accordingly.

Thanks to Prophetess Anita for bringing this book forth and her authenticity in the work for God. Keep doing those things that are pleasing in His sight.

Rev. J.A. Crawley
Former Pastor
New Jersey

PREFACE

God v. the state of the people

We have heard the opening statements from the prosecuting side on behalf of the world, now we will be hearing from the defense on behalf of Heaven. As I speak on the opening statement for the defense, that God is a Spirit from Eternity, the Alpha & Omega, beginning and the end. God who IS... has created, in the beginning {Genesis1:1} "And he said" "And he let there be" "And it was good." God who IS..."said let us" in our, after our, let them have. So God created, his word was fashioned, established, accomplished. After all that He is, has said, and has done, man has the audacity to still question his ability of who he is after seeing the evidence, enjoying the manifestation, and taking dominion over the works of His hands. This was God's gift to man so that he will benefit from as his creature and their creator.

Anyone who have thought man would be grateful be fruitful and multiply, but instead they chose to be unfaithful masterminds, trying to exclude God out of His plans, write him out of His will and insult His intelligence by trying to make him co-equal with their gods. This is the case of "then your eyes shall be opened, and ye shall be as gods knowing good and evil." {Genesis 3:5} Here with the evidence of God's handiwork, one still wants proof of His existence.

This book will prove by Heavens Certified Board under the penal code of Matthew 7:23, where the state of the people have continually maliciously represented God, for self-gratitude, self-indulgence, and selfishness. God is suing this nation for defamation of character. His name has been torn apart liken unto wolves who tear meat apart from their prey. I stand as the defense lawyer. I am here on God's behalf, to get His name back in the temple. The presence of God has been too long at Obed-Edom's house and it's time for us to go and get the Ark of Covenant back. I am here to defend an innocent God in an ungodly world. I'm here to give evidence of the report that has been proven that God is not bipolar; neither is He spiritually schizophrenic, the record will show that He holds the same weight from the beginning of time until the ending of time.

The records will show that God doesn't flow in and out of unfamiliar territory that will shift the functions of His assignment. Neither does He cause an unnecessary hurricane that will cause an extreme disturbance making God look as if disaster is part of His DNA. In this book we will find that God always keeps an even distribution of His Revelation of His own nature and His purpose for mankind.

WOLVES WHO WORSHIP

And he gave some, apostles; and some, prophets; and some, evangelists; and some, pastors and teachers; For the perfecting of the saints, for the work of the ministry, for the edifying of the body of Christ: Till we all come in the unity of the faith, and of the knowledge of the Son of God, unto a perfect man, unto the measure of the stature of the fullness of Christ: {Ephesians 4:11-13}

Jezebel has loosed the spirit of deception called" mystical enticement" where the Body of Christ is trying to be an "icon" as if the Church is an industry for Who is wise, and he shall understand these things?? Your degrees will not decipher, your title doesn't qualify, your rank will not grant you the results that the presence of God is so critical, without Him men will pray, but there will be no power, organs may play but the music will not compensate the soul choirs may sing, but no sweetness, the preacher will preach but the word will fall on thorny ground. Many will follow their evil teaching and shameful immorality. And because of these teachers, the way of truth will be slandered."{2 Peter 2:2} Beware of Satan's modern Philosophy called "seeker-sensitive" with false architects who have deliberately redesigned the worship service in order to make as few demands as possible on the person in the pew. They are throwing an artificial approach to the worship service by diminishing the proper place of preaching and replace it with quasi-spiritual forms of sheer entertainment. Any trend that threatens the centrality of God's Word in our corporate worship is a dangerous trend.

Separate yourselves from sensational seers, who are seekers of Satan determining abilities through their flesh by trying to perceive the present, forecast the future and predicting promotion without permission. "Your prophets courted you with sweet talk. They didn't face you with your sin so that you could repent. Their sermons were all wishful thinking, deceptive illusions."(Lamentations 2:14) The Devil has loosed his Ministering Magicians who are just practitioners that conjure up lukewarm praise with a contaminated worship, hired to only perform supernatural miracles with hypocritical power, your fairytale favor is mocking My glory, making my temple a play pit for fools, Your afflictions shall be greater than those of the heathens, ye shall fall into a snare, and when ye shall have gotten up ye shallfall again, I shall laugh at your calamity because your end is near REPENT AND RETURN. "The soul that shall go aside after magicians and soothsayers, and shall commit fornication with them, I will set my face against that soul, and destroy it out of the midst of its people." (Leviticus 20:6) THE MOUTH OF THE LORD HAS laughed at your calamity because your end is near, for the mouth of the LORD has spoken these things unto the Shepherds of his sheep, you have a desire to become popular to please man by pretending to preside over the people, but has become a predator with a poor posture lifting your filthy palms with a mouth full of petty prayers. "Your priests violated my law and desecrated my holy things. They can't tell the difference between sacred and secular. They tell people there's no difference between right and wrong. They're contemptuous of my holy Sabbaths, profaning me by trying to pull me down to their level. Your politicians are like wolves prowling and killing and rapaciously taking whatever they want. Your preachers cover up for the politicians by pretending to have received visions and special revelations. They say, "This is what God, the Master, says . . ." when God hasn't said so much as one word. Extortion is rife, robbery is epidemic, the poor and needy are abused, and outsiders are kicked around at will, with no access to justice."(Ezekiel 22:26)

God has loosed a WOE unto all those that want to take his agenda and make it yours; many are going out with the word that they have conjured up in the dark room of their mind, where you have become desperate to get the filthy lucre that you have deceived many from their lively hood. The spirit of deception is filling the streets like a stream, many are so hungry, they are panicking for a word of comfort, a word of peace, and a word that will release the stress. The wolves are now leading the feeble sheep away from the graze; they are preaching contradiction and making up their own doctrine. The wolves can see hunger in the eyes of the people, the wolves can smell desperation, the wolves can smell when one is not in fellowship with the Father, the wolves can smell when one doesn't understand the word of God, and the wolves can smell when one lives a hypocritical lifestyle. The wolves are now erecting buildings as decoys that are attractive, preaching catchphrases that will hook the attended target. The set up in the wolves cave is the same as in the church; the only way that you will know the difference is to have your discernment intensified. Wolves are professionals they know what to say, how to say it and where to say it, wolves calls revivals, one night prayer, conferences, and even use social media to catch over the web preys. Wolves who worship always need prey who doesn't pray, they look for people that are into the hype, they are looking for people that don't want to be taught, only want to be yelled at not taught to. Wolves love to go to a place where no real worship takes place. Wolves are presumptuous, everything they do is for an emotional demonstrations. To keep you from coming into the truth, wolves watch to make sure you don't get what you came to church for. Wolves are attracted to publicity where all eyes and advertisement speaks well of them. Wolves are very clever; they have an exquisite market strategy to promote business and boost sales. Wolves are excellent sales representatives, they take the word and try to sale it as a product, and sadly it has become successful. The open the bible and add up the numbers of the book, then multiply it by the verses and divide the sum among themselves. If they read 1 verse they will multiply that verse by the number of people in the sanctuary and call the number as in a bingo or on a scratch off. The people of God are losing their faith as the world's economics are scarce, so the hustle of the pyramid scams in the world has become old, now the new pyramid is starting in the five-fold. Each and every office in the five-fold are assembling together calling it a "gathering" but underneath it's the latter rain scam, where each office gives a general prophecy of the worlds system, the worlds leadership, the world's economic downfall, when in the word of God, Jesus says in Matthew 24 *"3 And as he sat upon the mount of Olives, the disciples came unto him privately, saying, Tell us, when shall these things be? and what shall be the sign of thy coming, and of the end of the world? 4 And Jesus answered and said unto them, Take heed that no man deceive you.5 For many shall come in my name, saying, I am Christ; and shall deceive many.6 And ye shall hear of wars and rumours of wars: see that ye be not troubled: for all these things must come to pass, but the end is not yet.7 For nation shall rise against nation, and kingdom against kingdom: and there shall be famines, and pestilences, and earthquakes, in divers places.8 All these are the beginning of sorrows. Then shall they deliver you up to be afflicted, and shall kill you: and ye shall be hated of all nations for my name's sake.10 And then shall many be offended, and shall betray one another, and shall hate one another.11 And many false prophets shall rise, and shall deceive many. 12 And because iniquity shall abound, the love of many shall wax cold.13 But he that shall endure unto the end, the same shall be saved."*

WOE UNTO YOU, who are ministers of the dark,

using your vessels as advocates between the living and dead, communicating to the grave souls trying to forth-tell the future...WOE UNTO YOU, who desires answers from the departed seeking information about tomorrow...WOE UNTO YOU, who participates in this rebellious ritual, I shall soon visit you, for you have neglected to seek me for answers, but consulted in the mediums who are frauds using their memory for tricks, planting accomplices and special effects having fooled the very elect, now are you confused and corrupted through demonic channeling...REPENT or "I will resolutely reject persons who dabble in the occult or traffic with mediums, prostituting themselves in their practices. I will cut them off from their people."(Leviticus 20:6)

HEAR YE OH MY PEOPLE, THE WORD OF THE LORD...These are times of uncertainty, where your title is not your testimony, your status doesn't bring you salvation, your rank will not qualify you for righteousness. TRUST NOT in this ever changing world who are the end-of-the-world manipulators, pressuring for instant profit with short-term ideas in the midst of chaos with a sign that says "we saved the world from disaster" You know as well as I that the day of the Master's coming can't be posted on our calendars. He won't call ahead and make an appointment any more than a burglar would. About the time everybody's walking around complacently, congratulating each other—"We've sure got it made! Now we can take it easy!"—suddenly everything will fall apart. It's going to come as suddenly and inescapably as birth pangs to a pregnant woman."{1 Thessalonians 5:3} WOE UNTO YOU Part-time Prophets who prophesy parched prophecies, only to parade around as a popinjay sounding like a parrot only to pacify the people, patching their sins, trying to repair their wickedness while producing false results...PRAY MY PEOPLE that ye may be found blameless, for when I shall come through with my rod of correction and my hand of judgment, PRAY that ye be spared from the snare of darkness and the hand of death. "And the prophets shall become wind, and the word is not in them: thus shall it be done unto them: (Jeremiah 5:13)

The Prophets prophesy falsely, and the priests bear rule by their means; and my people love to have it so: and what will ye do in the end thereof? (Jeremiah 5:31) GOD despises discord where the Body of Christ is separating into sub-divisions called exclusive societies with underground, ordinations undercover auditioning for the anointing, tryouts for Holy ghost power by preaching hidden message filled with philosophical theories. Know this "For God shall bring every work into judgment, with every secret thing, whether it be good, or whether it be evil." (Ecclesiastes 12:14) Signs of Satan's end-time Scam: He has sent out his sales representatives to offer freedom and self-sufficiency from an unreasonable God. He will make a humors laugh at sin, making light of it in comedian's routines, sitcoms, music and otherwise turning sin into a form of entertainment. He is anesthetizing the pain of guilt and sin by sending us teachers who tickle our ears making unrighteousness to be actually fine, even virtuous. He is singing the lullaby of presumption that consequences and judgment will not be our lot and with this lullaby we drift off into a moral sleep of indifference and false confidence. "Fake Messiahs and lying preachers are going to pop up everywhere. Their impressive credentials and dazzling performances will pull the wool over the eyes of even those who ought to know better. But I've given you fair warning.{Matthew 24:24} The Body of Christ has been infected by a backdoor beast called "The Trojan Horse" this spirit of sabotage masquerades as a patriot wearing a coat of loyalty. This hidden scavenger is maliciously programmed to undermine and exploit the downfall of its prey spreading spiritual decay, spiritual suicide and then death. Here is the prescription for this parasite, follow these instructions before destruction. "If my people, which are called by my name, shall humble themselves, and pray, and seek my face, and turn from their wicked ways; then will I hear from heaven, and will forgive their sin, and will heal their land."{2 Chronicles 7:14}

The end time exposure for the "influential five-fold" uncovering all secret orders, societies, and salutes to weighted down psychological jargon. Your ordinations have become nothing but an underhanded immoral operation, which exploits the ecclesiastical establishment. Your undisclosed meetings are in codes for the purpose of secrecy for Ministry money laundering, offering bribery, and bible extortion. Your conferences have turned into a Heresy Explosion a hazardous outbreak of apostasy. "Nevertheless I have somewhat against thee, because thou hast left thy first love. Remember therefore from whence thou art fallen, and repent, and do the first works; or else I will come unto thee quickly, and will remove thy candlestick out of his place, except thou repent." {Revelation 2:4-5} The church has become a consumer commodity bombarded by superficial service, goods, and materialism philosophy, adding futile methodologies to God's Word. At worst, such an attempt rejects the sufficiency of the Scriptures in favor of works of the flesh, quenches the Holy Spirit, and subjects one to the deceptions of, the service of, and in the end, the bondage of the god of this world. In any case, it leads to spiritual apostasy and biblical illiterates. "For what shall it profit a man, if he shall gain the whole world, and lose his own soul? Or what can anyone give in exchange for their soul?"{Mark 8:36-37}

Beware in this season of Satan's government structure called the fallacy fivefold ministry with angel of light doctrines; His organization consists of: apostate Apostles, pacifying Prophets, itching ear Evangelist, disloyal Pastors and heretical Teachers; thus placing the church on a false foundation, that is camouflaged in dictatorships, evil economic systems and the exploitation of the fear of man and the love of power. "No wonder, for even Satan disguises himself as an angel of light. Therefore it is not surprising if his servants also disguise themselves as servants of righteousness, whose end will be according to their deeds." {2 Corinthians 11:14-15} Watch out for Satan's special task force, armed forced set up to superficially resemble the Kingdom of God. This spirit knows its audience that encompasses seasonal saints, cultural casual and religious recipients. This special operation is to subtly soothe you with a hypnotic agent called "phraseology" a mix matching message by leaving out the Spirit of the Word. "For there shall arise false Christ, and false prophets, and shall shew great signs and wonders; insomuch that, if it were possible, they shall deceive the very elect."{Matthew 24:24}

The Lord is saying enough is enough! The Shepherds have used their positions to secure financial positions, the Prophets are seducing the multitudes for financial support, by using psychological and spiritual manipulation. ENOUGH IS ENOUGH, I can't stand your religious meetings. I'm fed up with your conferences and conventions. I want nothing to do with your religion projects, your pretentious slogans and goals. I'm sick of your fund-raising schemes, your public relations and image making. I've had all I can take of your noisy ego-music. When was the last time you sang to me? {Amos 5:21-24} REPENT AND LET US REASON TOGETHER SAITH THE LORD! The world has had far greater influence on our churches than our churches have had on the world. And while the world is getting worse and worse, the church has lost its voice to "Cry aloud, spare not, lift up thy voice like a trumpet, and shew my people their transgression, and the house of Jacob their sins."

Platform Prophets that love to perform in front of people who is of the carnal mind, these Prophets eyes see nothing and God has rejected their revelation for it's a preoccupied mystical of self worth ideas, only to point towards idol issues that is not consistent with the word of God, they have been disqualified and their mantles have been expired, they have no authority neither anointing because they have decided to change their concept of who God really is. These Prophets have selective hearing making mercenary their ministry to support their financial gain over the weakness of the sheep; they are using psychological and spiritual manipulation. (Micah 3:11)

Egos desire affirmation and delights in praises of the people serving the appetites of fallen man with a poor self-image called Pride. The formula for failure is self-glory and self gratification. We have become of a church where prophecy is a pep rally, which generates a great burst of shorter enthusiasm which does little to inspire faith and endurance in the midst of suffering, for this reason is because Satan is getting to much publicity, we have been advertising our adversity with the adversary by self-promoting the flesh branding our name to boost sales for the media and not the kingdom. As we stand in the compromise the Spiritual condition of the church has become corrupted. Why? Because many are so comfortable and gullible that they indiscriminately accept the pronouncements from the Prophets who are over-confident speaking from the belly of their own imagination called revelations of convenience, when one speaks from their own thoughts and opinions it's dangerous, when one pompously assumes a position or role without the endorsement of Heaven. Don't be deceived, being "self-appointed is the WORST example of carrying out God's will, remember replicas are never replaced they are removed, "The steps of a good man are ordered by the Lord: and he delighteth in his way."{Psalm 37:23} People in ministry especially in the public eye are more concerned with their reputation and popularity the pulpits and other places are filled with those liken unto Diotrephes one who loves to have first place, up front position, power and prestige. The Spirit of Diotrephes are operating in illegal authority Prophets who are always babbling trying to render prophecies through their own bias opinion is called "prophetic malpractice" be careful because their mantels have expired and out of their bellies is not a rhema word but just run on sentences. "Because a time will come when some will no longer tolerate sound teaching. Instead, they will live by their own desires; they'll scratch their itching ears by surrounding themselves with teachers who approve of their lifestyles and tell them what they want to hear. {2 Timothy 4:3}

We have to be very careful in the end time, because the devil has taken his place, and we as the People of God must take our place, the times are evil and we must redeem the time in a godly fashion. Some have turned away from the faith, they either are in the grave or contemplating suicide, our best recommendation is to stay in the secret place, of the most High will always abide forever. Satan is trying to make our minds as well as our bodies to agree with his plan, he is going to and fro even now more than ever, the very elect is he seeking to devour. We already have the key to eternal life, but we chose not to use it to unlock the doors that will save our lives. We keep changing the doors and using the key that doesn't fit, in the book of Genesis 6:3 "My Spirit shall not strive with man forever, because he also is flesh; nevertheless his days shall be one hundred and twenty years."

For the time is come that judgment must begin at the house of God: and if it first begin at us, what shall the end be of them that obey not the gospel of God? And if the righteous scarcely be saved, where shall the ungodly and the sinner appear? 1 Peter 4:17-18

The Lord is not slack concerning his promise, as some men count slackness; but is longsuffering to us-ward, not willing that any should perish, but that all should come to repentance. 2 Peter 3:9

GOD IS NOT A MAN

In Numbers 23:19 the bible lets us know that God is not a man that He should lie; neither the son of man, that he should repent: hath he said, and shall he not do it? Or hath he spoken, and shall he not make it good? Here is the descriptive evidence that God has a heavenly symmetry that God was not made from the dust, God has an inexplicable profusion of power. When He speaks the winds obey. When God speaks the thunder claps. When God speaks the trees bow at His presence. When God speaks the ocean gives way to His glory. He was not born of a woman, because no womb would have been able to hold the greatness of His majesty, no man's loins could have conceived power and glory. There is not a seed known to man that can ever pass into a woman that can produce anything close to God. God's footing is the balance to forever, His stability is the eyes to eternal, the unison of His ears is on one accord with the cries of the righteous, and the harmony of His voice is melodiousness with the heavenly host as they sing the hymn of holy.

God's prophetic equilibrium is so essential in these times of evil and wickedness, where there is confusion concerning the gospel; we find that there are more people walking away from God, than with God. Many believe that the promises of God are preposterous and obedience is not an option. These days, the church is not very high on the list of any significant institutions, because the church has slipped into a spirit of Ichabod, where the glory has departed. The church was indented to be a "HOLY NATION." The church has all the components of being a ROYAL PRIESTHOOD. My concern about the church is that we have become interested in the art of the church, that the church has become an ecclesiastical antique shop; we have abandoned His magnificent splendorous presence, and turned it into a down trodden faith of doctrines of devils. We no longer want to go behind the veil where we can encounter the presence of God, but instead we have birthed the spirit of Ishmael, wild and untamed, blind to the presence of God, no shame in His presence, no loyalty just out of debt with God but indebted to the world. Everyone is doing what is right in their own eyes, self-serving, egotistical, arrogant, pursuers of pleasure, rather than possessors of the cross. The devil has put up the perfect stage to perpetrate his "grand delusion."

This grand master deceiver has a three-legged plan of deception and is coming out of the woodwork with his own brand of "pop" psychology; deceiving even the elect. Satan has sent out his chief doctrinal saboteurs to deliberately dumb the truth to the lowest common denominator to appeal many with short attention spans. He has created an upside down floor plan where the Church now needs props and prompts when to and how to. We have become robots with a mechanical praise. Instead of preparing for the future they will be preparing for the funeral. God existed before the thought of mankind could ever conceive as much. God is never without the sum or a total, and He never has to carry over or cancel out, because of too much or not enough. God doesn't need a chart of how to connect with a result of never coming to a balance that has to end according to the earth's format. God is not broken down to the lowest common denominator; God is not divided, the Heavenly Host will not cause confusion, but they will synchronize with the hymnologist, the Cherubim and Seraphim as they sing the Anthem of Heaven, "Holy, Holy, Holy". od subtracts without taking away and adds without having an answer key. He multiplies through equations that equals only to what has never been before. God pulls the weight and depth out of Himself. God has volumes of widths that exceeds beyond the scientist metric system, their theories always make God seem as though He has fallen short. Their theories always leave a balance, where the outcome has a remainder and the equation will always be incomplete.

God's equilibrium is attached to Philippians 1:6 Being confident of this very thing, that he which hath begun a good work in you will perform it until the day of Jesus Christ: The balance sheet of heaven always totals out to "exceeding abundantly above all we can ask or think." The word all is the total amount extending to the greatest amount, nothing lacking because of "leftovers" that can't be solved. Man's promises will always fall short because their heart is wicked. God is the whole amount of summation that is undivided, unabbreviated and unexpurgated. God's equilibrium is faultless, His power plus His strength equals a dunamis authority as the balance. God stands in agreement with His knowledge which activates a harmonious union by sending a sound that is in harmony with His word and His will, binding together the beginning and the end. While man must manipulate symbols, move the decimal, take away and carry the digits. Being pompous, man borrows from the greatest figure hoping to round off to the nearest place value, which has no value because the equation is falsely balanced. They have all sorts of calculations to try to put together the end results, because of this failure man will continue to have their own opinions and speculation which will result in a mass accumulation of chaos causing a crash in statement and transactions.

God doesn't need man's formula in order for Him to be captured as God in the lens of man's eyes. In this journey man will always struggle trying to find out what makes God, God, that's why they will always have a subtotal and never a zero balance. For here is the great effort on their behalf of this appalling and horrible thing that is continuing to happen in the land. Apostles have become Apostates, the Church is chasing these muppet performing Prophets like the paparazzi, Pastors are building crouton crowds and preaching these side-splitting sermons glossed over with gospel gimmicks, the Evangelist is going to and fro as illusionist mediums delivering messages of deception, and Teachers are using self-help books to supplement the Bible. WAKE UP!

"For the time is come that judgment must begin at the house of God: and if it first begin at us, what shall the end be of them that obey not the gospel of God?"{1 Peter 4:17}

God's mind is not irregular that His eye sight is short spanned that He does not see the treacherous prophets that are prophesying from a dark pit, just a circus full of gospel gamblers where miracles depend on money, where man is prostituting promises... believing these who stand boldly pulling on heavens handle to find a word of wealth reaping coins of corruption filled with change of calamity. The mind of man has become lopsided, where he has forgotten "it is he that has made us, and not we ourselves" and now the Saints have become superstars, the Church has become a television stage, the people are changing characters to act out the anointing.

Programs bind the presence of God and the service is directed by cue cards. So when we begin to go against the plan of God, men will pray, but there will be no power, organs may play but no sweetness, choirs may sing but the music will not compensate the soul. The preacher will preach but the word will fall on thorny ground. Without the true equilibrium of God, we can build it, but God has to put His benediction on it. We can design it but God has to dedicate it. We can structure it, but God has to sanctify it. We can plan it, but God has to purify it. The brick mason put it together with mortar, but God put it together with mercy, the mines provided the stones, but God is the Chief Cornerstone. The contractor worked by blueprints, but God had a divine design. The structure is welded steel, but the Superstructure is the plan of salvation. Because of God's Prophetic Equilibrium, the engineer studied the strength of the structure, "before the hills in order stood, long before the earth received her frame!"

The draftsmen said, "Build it on the rock foundation." The architect wrote up the specifications, but God asked the architect a question: "Where were you when I unrolled the foundation of the earth? Where were you when I hitched it to nothing and fastened it with my word? Where were you when I gave the wind its breath, when I shot the stars as a million skyrockets, when I scattered the fleecy white clouds against the bosom of the blue, when I took a lump of clay and made man out of dust, stamped my image on his brow, put the quest of truth in his heart, and divinity in his soul. Furthermore, where were you when the morning stars sang together and the sons of God shouted for joy? {Scripture in Job}

Man will still struggle with being unstable because competition has penetrated the church to the extent that many churches approach ministry like a sports event. They view their mission as a business that seeks to gain market share among Christians—donors, members, influence—all under the name of God. This pathway of destruction through antagonisms, resentments, profane babblings and other perversions within His Body have developed a institution called "Opinionated Churches of Christ." Here is where many claim to trust in the word of God alone while going to their "expert scholars" as a substitute for the doctrine of Christ which causes the Body to digress into the headquarters of indoctrination. "Now I beseech you, brethren, mark them which cause divisions and offences contrary to the doctrine which ye have learned; and avoid them."{Romans 16:17}

The church has been weighed in the balance and found wanting, they have exchanged the truth for a feel-good-faith called "soul preaching." It is a scheme used with scripture to reason with the flesh so man will not obey the will of God. It is like a cancer inside the body that has been spreading by uncontrolled opinions that are overused and betrayed by lack of original thoughts. This results in secret exclusions, making one think they have been denied access to the promise. They are without relationship with Christ and preaching their own philosophy, persuading many false visionary speculations that are unrealistic, making God's Prophetic Equilibrium a three headed beast. We all know so well that there is no such thing as equilibrium would be out of stability, But God hath chosen the foolish things of the world to confound the wise; and God hath chosen the weak things of the world to confound the things which are mighty; {1 Corinthians 1:27}. You cannot clone God's greatness because there's no genetic makeup, there isn't a blood sample available to prove that there is no one before

Him or after Him. Scientists will be humanly deprived and mentally lacking the fundamentals of God's divine nature. They will constantly struggle with the fact that they cannot trace God back to any man. How quickly they forgot that "In the beginning God created" {Genesis 1:1} Mankind has been constantly developing their own equation, for this reason, the wicked says "there is no God." In addition, man will create whatever they want; works protected with a password of "do your own thing" but his journey will only end with death by self-destruction. "Only fools say in their hearts, "There is no God." They are corrupt, and their actions are evil; not one of them does good!"(Psalm 14:1). God's form cannot be duplicated, the blueprint of His glory, it's a reproduction of heaven in an earthly layout. All of the measurements are equally balanced on every side making it perfect in all dimensions. All the of the mathematics are so precise, there are no adjustments, modifications, fluctuations or corrections, even though the height and depth of the mercy of God is still without limitations.

His caliber gives us a great return on our investment, no number will be outstanding, the figure of favor is innumerable, and the quantity of God's blessings will never be on demand because there is enough for everyone to receive their portion. The facility of God's uniform is never off scale. He never compromises the weight of His glory because it's incompatible, never to sync or become paired with another device by a manufactured manual so that you can download and put as a shortcut on your home screen.

The trichotomy of God's Prophetic cannot be separated into categories, all of His qualities and characteristics are not voice-activated commands but His Excellency is preeminent and His holiness is still in high rank, contrary to popular opinion HOLINESS IS STILL RIGHT AND REQUIRED.

GOD'S SUPERNATURAL TRICHOTOMY

Father, Son & Holy Spirit

God never changes His heavenly attire; He is fully clothed in righteousness, holiness, and godliness. There is no division in God's standards. God works out of the normal yet He is elevated over the ordinary. God will not go outside of His original unchanging nature, because He has a permanent garment of glory. God has a consistent clothing line of supreme splendor. God walks in the oneness of greatness, and He speaks in eternal excellence, He sits in regal and royal power. God's holiness makes the sea behave, the tree's bend and cry holy, makes the sand and its constituents give up the depths of its surface. He makes the seed in the ground yield its increase, and makes the moon give light in eternity and in the earth both at the same time.

That is why people who are of the true vine, must wear God's trichotomy. The temperature of God's supernatural thermometer will not have you chemically unbalanced because He is neither hot nor cold but equally high above all, without boundaries, limitations and dimension. This uniform starts from the root of righteousness. No flesh can alter this infinite God; no one can put God inside a box for His heavenly host must cry holy, holy, holy because of His majestic glory. The power that God possesses is exceeding intricate, any attempt to formulate or to stamp a dogma on His itinerary becomes a sham, fraught with pretension. God's ways are just, right, and wise. God is not like man He is not resistant to misunderstanding, yet God's ways often stuns man's power, making Him unequivocal to the wisdom of God.

God's uniform is tailor made to fit your troubles, there is no greater problem that ever dares to compete with God's power; He has an extensive plan that's not expensive. Once God invents it, NO man can prevent it, the devil will object, but God will overrule and super rule. The devil has been spreading false reports, holiness still has standards, miracles are not a mystery, your vision is not dead but sleep, go and wake it up, your promise still has a pulse. The dry bones in Ezekiel describe the trichotomy of the bones, God being the chief doctor, saw passed the flesh and saw life in them. Dry doesn't mean that it's over for you; it's just lacking life, lacking hope, and lacking the fullness of God's equilibrium.

Satan is trying to dismember the Body of Christ by cutting out the Five-Fold function, replacing it with synthetic salvation, with the mockery of man-made titles making the body unfit for use, He wants to divide the people into pieces making the Church look like a three headed beast. What Satan fails to realize is that God's uniform cannot be cloned, His caliber gives you a return on your investment, and His righteousness is still in high rank. One cannot separate God into categories, all His qualities and characteristics sync together, his Excellency is preeminent. The faculty of God's uniform is never off balance, God will never compromise his trichotomy his uniform is not compatible to any other features because it will hinder the flow of holiness which is so forever present. The garments of God are perfectly detailed to fit the dimensions of the mercy seat; it covers His matchless deity, his incomparable glory, and the picture-perfect presence of God. The transaction of God's trichotomy is nonnegotiable His strength cannot be bargained for, His revelation is not a business deal and His grace is not an exchange for cash. The dichotomy of God is his Grace and Mercy. God's grace is an expensive fragrance that through the oil and water, causes stabilization and protection for the faithful.

Grace is a converter containing a high level of power in exchange for heaviness. Grace is a chasing agent that eliminates disturbance from its regular normal function. This grace agent stops all confusion and disorder, grace restores one back to its original state never to return or revisit. Grace is preparation to prevent attacks that can change complicated places that end in destruction and death as a result.

Mercy is a large structured mansion with many quarters. Each room accommodates forgiveness, kindness and liberality; each chamber holds an innumerable amount of equivalency. Too numerous to be counted, but one knows it's available without limit, without walls making it sufficient, available and appropriate for any position, post or status. It's designed to fit the need to the extent that all areas are covered. The Trichotomy of God's grace and mercy is John 3:16 For God so loved the world, that he gave his only begotten Son, that whosoever believeth in him should not perish, but have everlasting life. 'God loved,' is the liaison to maintain His word with his people. 'Gave' is the uncommon compensation without expecting a return, and 'life' is a forever anatomy that never ceases from offering or administering into a place where God lives and dwell eternally.

THE NATURAL BALANCE OF GOD'S EYES, EARS & HANDS

From the human's position the natural eye's purpose is to see only what the natural eye can allow you to see. With our eyes we have to adjust to the appearances of people's shapes and positions. Our eyes can only carry what the muscle can stretch beyond, which is just limited without making us blind. The human eye must go through the cycle of eye conditions in order for them to retain their 20/20 vision, some lose and some never changes, but the eye is not built for longevity, it must go through the slideshows of the degeneration and deterioration. Then the human eye goes through segregation, where what use to function cannot accommodate the lenses to help clear the vision in order to see, and this is where blindness makes it grand appearance.

The imperceptions of the eye are very dangerous; it attracts strange undiscerning paths that can lead to death. When you are deprived from seeing, then you lean to your own understanding and won't be able to enjoy the proficiency of the Master's eternal consistent source, you will not be able to grasp the greatness that is stored behind what the human eye cannot ever perceive. The eyes are very important to the body; God has designed in the natural as well as the spiritual to give us an advantage of the adversary. Our Spiritual eye is already ordained to see what God sees and in the spiritual realm. Our eyes have daily dialogue with the eyes of the LORD; He has to adjust our pupils to heavens glory making sure our minds have been mounted up so our eyes can behold Him. God's eyes are exempt to man's misunderstanding, yet man will never comprehend. What becomes undeniable in God's eyes is vague in man's intelligence. His eyes detect the very inner part of your heart, when you go behind the veil there is a mirror that God reveals to you, to show you just who you are, your motives and moves.

The trichotomy of God's supernatural eyes is holiness, righteous and godliness, when you come into the presence of God, He will see the defect, your fault and the flaw. God's eyes are equipped to catch what man tries to hide; God navigates straight through the fictitious intentions that will cause to portray dishonorable double-dealing. God's eyes see past the image that man so easy builds in their finite mind, where the image of wood that neither see, nor saves, the silver or gold that neither satisfies nor edifies. God's eyes are equipped to catch the very thing that man tries to hide. God's eyes navigate straight through the fictitious intentions of man's heart "The heart is deceitful above all things, and desperately wicked: who can know it? {Jeremiah 17:9} The superstructure of God's eyes submerges the outer layer and goes beyond the limits of man's intellect, man cannot expand his mind pass the permission and the ability of God. While man's eyes are full of all that is in the world, the lust of the flesh, and the lust of the eyes, and the pride of life, man has forgotten that God's eyes are in every place beholding the evil and the good. {Proverb 15:3} God's eyes look while the world desires riches, He desires righteousness, the world desires fornication, God desires faithfulness, the world desires rituals, God desires relationship, the world desires tradition, God desires truthfulness, and while the world desires to war, God says worship. The watchman is put on the wall as an examiner, but because men love the dark rather than the light, they have become an exterminator for the enemy.

As a result of the wrongdoing that has been embedded into the inner chamber of the center of the heart, God's eyes are equipped to catch the evil that so dominates our actions. From the throne God is looking at this big damage control campaign going on, called "The Spirit of Perversion." This body possessor is a moral failure in the Body of Christ and has become an epidemic. This spirit's two main weapons attracts false teachers, false doctrines, which results in false teachings. Its main objective is to create the center of attention to its master Jezebel, the priestess of Baal. This spirit attacks the Church through defiled pulpits that have an insatiable appetite. The pulpits that have open themselves up to containers of unclean spirits spreading and corrupting the whole Body of Christ. Make no mistake about it, this spirit is more common than any other spirit in existence. "Lust gets pregnant, and has a baby: sin! Sin grows up to adulthood, and becomes a real killer."{James 1:15}

In the seat of the eye is called the chamber of light. In this tabernacle the eye is important; the area where the oil of the anointing drains the eyes of deception. In this tabernacle is the mercy seat where the eye sits and pours out the oil to drain the eyes from all of the world's wickedness. The eyes have to be properly drained daily, releasing the buildup causing a blockage in the opening gate of the eye. Without this cleansing the portal of the eye will become damaged and the wall dividing the veil will cloud the interpretation nerve, where man is able to see in the supernatural. This nerve is essential and helps intensify the discernment of what man sees. This view is attached into the muscle and strengthens the eye of interpretation. The view vein expands the eye so that it will release interpretation, verification, and appraisal report, inspect and confirm.

The interpretation of the eye is the audit adjuster; the verification is the eye endorser, the appraisal report where the eye releases a survey. The eye inspector is the superintendent of surveillance, it searches the parameters for the truth to confirm and establish that accuracy in order to administer affirmation.

The eye is the legwork to understanding; it travels intensively collecting, correcting and confirming what the eye receives. This is the equal net, the base and framework to balance the "eye-sheet" for publication and it can be printed to see the now or what is to come in an undisputable view. This helps the eye get a glimpse beforehand as to what is real or counterfeit. The eye has its own patent that protects thieves from the original copyright that has been sealed since the beginning of time, each range of vision is under heaven's disclosure, the eye can't go into bankruptcy because the blue print of the eye belongs to God. It is given to delegates as an "eyescape" each member has a complete layout that is full of revelation, authentication and declaration, only the eye is able to detect the unknown, validation, and decree. The anatomy of the eye is the compass cardinal of the lens, which consists of the north eye, the south eye, the east eye, and the west eye. The north eye is the audit adjuster. This compass faces the north because it has the power to switch, being responsible to generate a diaphanous tissue that makes all angles of the eye approachable without threat. The south eye is the docking port that is station near the harbor. This socket is called the anchor; it has to hold the foundation of the eye with security protection and providence.

Without the foundation the support of the socket will lose its attachments that are responsible for pulling the viewer to the inner vision in order for one to see past, present and future. The north eye is the arctic of the eye, a watchtower that faces eternally towards the tip where the eye can get a clear glimpse of God without complicated distractions, deception and dishonesty. The eye is a witness to what needs to be seen in order for one to make good judgment. The eye is the veil that keeps out destruction, overcast and darkness. The mist of the eye is the visibility of victory this allows one to look into faith and see it happening before it manifest. The east of this compass is the "pupil of prophecy" this allows the eye to look towards the son, for their redemption draws nigh. This lens foretells the "evidence not seen" the pupil carries the weight of the promises that have been spoken but yet manifested, the pupil can predict what no other parts of the body can imagine, the pupil gets a first gland of things to come. The verification is the eye endorser. It issues a warrant to arrest all false information with fictitious credentials. The eye of verification checks out things ahead of time to keep from having bounced check prophecies.

The eyes have a prominent seat in the pupil, it is the testimonial towered that is fortified by faith. This high rise allows the believer to look beyond what's to come, when the eye has not looked forward first, then it leaves the main vein of the eye open for attack, which will cause blindness. That is where the eye report generates a preplan summary that prints out a statement balance; this function manifests what was seen or what is said to come. It's responsible to dispatch the anatomy for danger, and this report warns the pending threat. The heart of the eye is the author of multiple manifestations of demonstrations; liken unto Moses and the red sea, God instructed Moses to look (see) what's in his hand, he moved his pupil towards the prophecy and as he believed God the sea opened up. These three conduits help the eye see the impossible, the appearance (the burning bush), the demonstration (red sea), and the representation (I AM the I AM).

The appraisal eye is a costly gem, a precious rare optical. The appraisal of the eye is a treasure, a macroscopic masterpiece that is part of the eye elite which is the headlight to holiness. Not everyone possess this gem because the elite is powerful and holds authority and is the capital of the eyelift. The eyelift reduces bad perceptions and cloudy vision, it's an advancement that clears the view for any critical hindrances such as misalignments. In this chamber lift comes the crescendo power that has full coverage with a no fault policy. This package protects from the sensitivity of a false insight that expands impossibilities and reroutes what God has already manifested to a person in the previous prophecy.

When the eyes travel by means of looking out of the alignment the eye falls into a world called pride, which changes the light of the eyes to a stain pigment that is the color of self-fulfillment and self-satisfaction. The eye inspection searches unlimited supply of source and strength, it takes inventory to observe what is needed and what's not. Sometimes the eye can be weighed down with unnecessary information. The eye lifter has to illustrate a schedule or an agenda only by the voice of God where he will give a clear indication that the eye has stored up funds that have resources such as assets and availability that one can see only with permission. This is where the special fund comes into play as the access key to

Psalm 121, "I will look to the hills" as the password.

This eye connection to the cliff of the bank is where the eyes will receive revenue that will maintain in the weakest point, yet sharpen the eye image keeping it from depleting the field of fulfillment where the vision will not be poverty stricken, where the eye will slowly slip into a place of "purblind" slow, impaired where discernment no longer exist. The eye is the superintendent of surveillance, because it confirms the truth, establishes accuracy and administers affirmation. Only the eye can go ahead, see and stop the incoming activity that will infiltrate the eyes from seeing manifestation. Your eyes are a very intricate part of the body, God knew where to place this globular organ, and deposit the assignment in which the lining of the veil of the eye will allow all mankind to view the world's anatomy and enjoy God's handiwork.

THE BALANCE OF GOD'S EARS

One thing is certain, God hears everything that moves, breathes and has their being. God is fed-up with what He has been hearing. How did we ever get such man-pleasing leaders? All of the old ancients have been destroyed before our very eyes and hardly a peep from the pulpit. They are called pulpit puppets one who just sits and is moved by model performance, they sit and hear wrong and keep silent. They are not concerned about the matters that goes on within the fold, for the sheep has gone astray because the Shepherd has no voice. The pasture is no longer a concern they have replaced it with their position that they have brought from dishonest scant vendors "A false balance is abomination to the LORD: but a just weight is his delight." {Proverbs 1:1}

In the book of Micah 6:12 "For the rich men thereof are full of violence, and the inhabitants thereof have spoken lies, and their tongue is deceitful in their mouth" They have the notion that all power is behind their cross and credentials, they can cast out demons according to their clergy collar, their vestment will determine their victory. They sit back with the spirit of arrival, while the church is dying. This silence comes from being in the presence of learned behavior which produces the recycling of more mouthpiece minions who have become muzzled because it is prohibited to break the code of silence. Some will rather fall then fight. "That they may do evil with both hands earnestly, the prince asketh and the judge asketh for a reward; and the great man, he uttereth his mischievous desire: so they wrap it up." {Micah 7:3} God heard the cries of Cain's brother from the ground "the voice of thy brother's blood crieth unto me from the ground." {Genesis 4:10} God hears all the whispers of the wicked; even when they call themselves lip syncing. He hears all background noises of those that have premeditated prayer that is only for display for public theatrics with lengthy words and symptoms of repetition. Falsely dressed in servant attire and are simply sneaky religious backseat bystanders that are not doers of the word but just churchgoers looking for front seat praise to grandstand. They only seek to attract attention and applause by conspicuous behavior as one viewing the service as a sporting event with VIP seating. Their lives are perpetual fashion shows, embroidered prayer shawls one day and flowery prayers the next. They love to sit at the head table at church dinners, basking in the most prominent positions, preening in the radiance of public flattery, receiving honorary degrees, and getting called 'Doctor' and 'Reverend.' {Matthew 23:5-7 msg}

God hears the scams of Satan's end time schemes, He has sent out his sales representatives to offer freedom and self-sufficiency from an unreasonable God. He will make a humorous laugh at sin, making light of it in comedian's routines, sitcoms, music and otherwise turning sin into a form of entertainment. He is anesthetizing the pain of guilt and sin by sending us teachers who tickle our ears making unrighteousness to be actually acceptable, even virtuous. He is singing the lullaby of presumption that consequences and judgment will not be our lot and with this lullaby we drift off into a moral sleep of indifference and false confidence. "Fake Messiahs and lying preachers are going to pop up everywhere. Their impressive credentials and dazzling performances will pull the wool over the eyes of even those who ought to know better. But I've given you fair warning. {Matthew 24:24}

The ear is a deep and undisturbed sound that plays in the midst of the tabernacle. The ear is the instrumentalist that combines the sound string, the wood in the wind; the brass is the blessings of the believer and the percussion of Pentecost. The external part of the ear is auricle, where the lug is the hangings and the lobe is the power portion that supports all the sounds making sure that nothing enters to damage the sound from heaven. The lobe is the protection from the growls of the wicked one. The ear is the prominence that stands in front of all negative vibrations that travel through the air looking for a landing deck to release pressure into the receptive vein. The ear has an internal auscultation, which is the base where the wind of the sound will inform the listening tube to tune into airtime from heaven, where there is a 24 hour wireless WIFI broadcast. This wireless attachment is connected to the throne so one that is available will catch and discover that God is getting ready to talk to His people. The ear is the head of the entry gate to the listening quarters for the "acoustic " where the inner tube will be able to catch a clear station to access the unsullied voice of God. In this inner tube is the trumpet, an instrument that alerts the drum of the ear to watch the intake. This sharp indicator implements a halcyon scent that clears the pathway for a low pitch and low toned that will lead to a sign that says "out of hearing."

In the inner courts of this acoustic sound it releases a clear clarion that will alarm the hearer either of danger or prayer. In this tabernacle of the ear is the altar, in this sacred chamber is where the prayers of the righteous are heard, the devil is apprehended, and His people can triumph in victory. The inner ear is the inner court where its filled with "hemoglobin" blood where the power is responsible for transporting the oil into the bodies that cry loud and spare not. This hemoglobin blood will strengthen the minds and the will of the saints given them the ability to mount up on wings as eagles. This process where the fluid must flow is vital to keep hazardous sounds out and dunamis fluids to flow back into the altar of the ear. This process will keep the ear full of consecration smearing on the life of the believer and its generations to come. The tabernacle of the ear has an outer layer that facilitates the hand of the ear to help move the deafening from a distant range to a clear-cut sound within reach. This activity promotes a distinctive and audible sound that alerts the host of the hearing assembly as they gather on one accord to cover close and beyond even to the most high extreme threat. The believer is responsible to watch what they hear outside of the furthermost, all the way to the aftermost, even beyond distance and behind. The ear is the most crucial part of the anatomy; this trichotomy informs all dangers to come and exposure to high level impending danger. Through this three level balance, the sound funnel provides the outermost vessel, which is the pathway that provides the means to get the picture clear to hear. The outward funnel helps move the ear to understand by receiving what is said, judging the words by closely watching the sounds that is considered to be visible portions of understanding. The final is the latter most which is the faith funnel, hearing it in times past of what God said, yet no manifestation. Yet the word is resonated deep down in a holding place of the ear, to remind the spirit of the ear, that what you heard will come to pass, no other word or confirmation can share this space, there is no space here for doubt, or reasoning. This special funnel can only hold one and that's the truth. The ear is the chief instrument that has keys to unlock all doors to receiving; this door holds reservations only to the truth. This key reserves the provison which is the clause without limitation terms and conditions, this key is not to take and unlock the unknown, but it's to admit the subscriber that is a ink supporter. The one who writes what God says and he that hears can understand it.

In the admittance chamber of company, the

witness of the truth becomes the beneficiary, the one who is the heir of annuity; they become the shareholder to the benefits, the progeny of the estate. This is allotted to all hearers as a reward for lending their ear to the voice of God. This gives you access to the kingdom of God that will come forth in the fullness of time, and be presented as a cloud recipient, the heritance of the saints and a array of the army of the Lord. The ways and means of this instrument is secured, guaranteed, and established. The tabernacle of the ear is a fixed set in the heavens. The benefits to the hearer, that the deposits are immovable. It's a legal tender where the abode of the blessed will have access to the Kingdom Trust Company, where the transfers of blessings is a nonstop wireless connection from the eternal conductor to the saints of the most high.

This daily day-to-day data is from the firmament fund. It's an advocate that is ordained to release resources such as riches, harvest and wealth from the thread in the auricle of the vein of the ear. It will cause one to hear, reap the accrual, gain the earnings and holdings due to the investor. The investor now through the ear can obtain and take dominion to expand and become qualified to be profitable for economic sufficiency. They will have more than enough from their gross so they can glean and live in the overflow. The investors are now entitled through the treasure fund of Heaven. They will now be able to reap the whole sum with no deductions and the vault of heaven will become their 24-hour ATM, the strong room, and the counting house.

The listening ear can grant you through portals of heaven. The ear is crucial, it introduces you to unlimited deposits called "income from obedience" this will allow you to withdrawal at anytime, where one can use their check with Psalm 23, use a withdrawal slip from the savings account that says Philippians 4:19, and the investor can use the withdrawal slip from the checking account with check number Luke 6:38. In the Bank of Heaven the tellers will approve it with the signature from the CEO with the stamp of Genesis 1:1 and John 1:1. Then the heavenly host tellers will give you a balance of 2 Corinthians 8:14. At the present time your plenty will supply what they need, so that in turn their plenty will supply what you need. The goal is equality. The surplus is unconsumed, nothing leftover horizontally or vertically, the formula can't be broken or disturbed, but give a net worth of "FAVOR" with a capitol of "BLESSINGS" and a savings net worth of "WEALTH"

THE ANATOMY OF GOD'S ANOINTING

The Supernatural Trichotomy of Structure

God's supernatural anatomy is beyond the superficial confinement of man's mind. The mind of man has always been limited because of the reprogramming from sin, sin being the major chaos up of our makeup. Scientist will continue to struggle because their understanding is unaided by the guidance of God. Their minds have become their god, because man has been taught to think with their own reason, and that their reason must come from what they see, and what they see must perceive to be true. Man's perception of God is just a figment of his imagination if he cannot see it or touch it, the world calls it fantasy, but we call it faith {Hebrews 11:1} God's composite is a structure that is eternal and timeless, God is without end and beginning. His framework is built with infinite ingredients that flow from the inner chamber of his glory, where the fragrance from the secret place is to the utmost degree of His splendor.

The Greatness of God's anatomy is His reputation; the name above all names is how we make our boast in Him. For His wisdom precedes any orchestrated theory, His sovereignty rules and super rules; His love goes beyond any greater than, without any expectations. God is self-existent, self-sufficient nothing in the universe is self-caused. God is perfect; there is no remainder or anything to carryover. There is no trace of His beginning or ending. His DNA cannot be found; the trace of anything human, any remains, there is no evidence of God's onset and off set. God's make-up cannot be made-up, it can't be duplicated, it's not a rough draft neither is He incomplete. God's anatomy is perfect, providing the appropriate parts for the human needs. God's anatomy is holiness, godliness, and righteousness, these three say, "and it was good, let us and let there be"

The Heavenly Laboratory

This lab is not an industry but it's a chamber that is incapable of fallacy. In this chamber is an eternal presence that forms an axial in the midst of the anointing combining an all-in-one source that is active daily for withdrawal; to circulate a continuous current. It's a preordained establishment to hold provision with a steadfast supply and a constant demand. This endless edifice holds fascinate fiber that aids the oil to flow freely into the tubes of righteousness, which solidifies the junction between justification and sanctification. This allows Christ to surround and expand the oil that flows from the theocratic throne where the center of His glory meets God's weight with the summary of His BMI, which is the Balance, Might and Impact of His glory. These three are synced together to form the diadem giving the anointing the authority to work between heaven and earth. Here we have a climactic event that is extremely detrimental to the lives of the believer. This major nerve determines the reasoning, the wisdom, and proficiency in the encephalon system, which is the "MIND." This is the ark, the safe place and the vessel by which man chooses to do right or wrong, to live holy or immoral, to be righteous or corrupt. The mind is where you have to make a decision of the actions that you must take towards and understand that there is no grey areas in the mind. The mind is the ark that carries your options and your consequences; this is the main vessel that has the verdict of life and death. The mind is an instrument that releases recommendations on how you govern yourself accordingly. In addition it is the how one must have order that "if you do" which is the curtain that lifts to life, God saying "then I will" which is the veil to everlasting life.

It is the benefits to taking possessions. The veil is the front cover that protects the sound mind from false fronts; it shields the mind from congestion of thoughts, by shutting off the blockage with the road sign that says there is a checkpoint ahead, do not proceed. This checkpoint is to prevent from reentering or accepting solicitations from satan and his sales people, or even receiving calls from the telemarketers of hell, calling to sell over priced services that have been already given for free at Calvary. These telemarketers have their own agendas to prostitute the people of God with a high price for the finest words, tricking them that they have the key to eternal life with a price. These sales people have unwarranted persuasions that demand outside harassments from lifetime hackers. They hustle to con the mind out of the safety. Their job is to sell unwanted products that will damage the mind causing a disorder with a vegetative state, where one becomes a patient with a severe brain damage walking around with side effects of long-term comatose uttering like a fool in Psalm 14:1 "there is no God;" going to and fro looking to find accusations about who created them. This syndrome happens to prevent one from becoming future followers and destiny walkers. The mind is set up to receive from the one that holds all power in his hand, but God in all of His awesomeness gives us a choice to receive him, for he only gives us the best, making sure that his people have first choice to the promise. However, the mind of mankind has fallen short of the glory of God, so God in his love for us sent the best gift of them all to redeem our minds back to where we can have fellowship with Father at no cost to us.

The ark of the mind has a balance sheet where we can be authorized, to become certified so we can testify. The balance sheet of the mind prints out the authorization to give birth to the relationship we have with God. God certifies us, that we have the power to bring into existence all that we experience at the hand of God, for example, healing, deliverance, miracles signs and wonders, so that we can testify about the mighty acts of God. God uses this balance sheet so that we may ACT on his behalf by staying in the Ark, continuing with the Covenant, and walking in truth. The mind epitomizes the eternal seal that empowers the mind to carry through and bring it to pass. For the ark is fully loaded stocked with sufficient funds of favor and peace for those who keep their minds stayed on Him. It's always loaded with provision and in reach for the believer. The mind is the bank's storehouse, with savings accumulating with promises, treasures, wealth, and continual prosperity. The harvest is loaded with abundance in riches and rewards that are automatically transferred over into the main portal of the brain where it instantly is available to those who have chosen to make Jesus their Lord and Savior.

In the mind is the seat of the senses where the eyes of the mind can see the proceeds of their prayers coming into fruition. The hand of the mind can have access to the annuity from the clapping of in praise. The ears of the mind can hear the report of the Lord when the doctor can't see beyond the balance of your healing at the bottom line. The feet of the mind takes and transports you into the presence of God when you can stand before God making your request known unto Him and stay until the breakthrough brook becomes a flood of endorsements that have been sitting and now must be manifested. In this secret place of Psalm 91, God is able to do a transformation on those who choose to abide under the shadow of the most High and they get to experience Romans 12:1 a living sacrifice. You are allowing God to reconstruct the cranium. This sensitive part is the base, the starter kit with basic instructions that has already been given to you in order that you may live, and exist. The cranium supernaturally holds the middlemost and the innermost characteristics of God. It's fully loaded with ammunition to believe, anticipate, reflect, and to estimate the value of gaining God, and the loss of losing God. The cranium is the hard shell that provides both support and protection, if not stabilized it will shift the bone and you can become paralyzed, stuck with more of the weight on the wrong side then the right side. The cranium is a supreme structure; the highest-ranking anatomy that cannot be compared to any other anatomy.

The supernatural of this formation is a complex composite yet simple enough to identify the faculties of God beyond the theory of the scientist circulatory system. This boneless prototype helps us to understand the beginning of Genesis "in the beginning God created," where God institutes the helmet of Salvation, which is the protector of mankind's mind. This helmet is a shell, hard padded with "LIFE" and the metal of mercy, the leather of loyalty and the plastic of power. For this reason God lets us know through this that all power belongs to him. The archeologist has no evidence to show how this cranium can be loaded with all of the fundamentals that keeps life alive. This superstructure of the blueprint explains the utterance of God in His holy word "Let us make man in our image, after our likeness:" God had "us" on his mind. God created us in the darkroom of creation, from the negative void of the earth. The helmet of Salvation keeps us connected to the power source at all times, the gallery that is on God's mind is pictures of His people, He puts us in high ranking status of the "let us" elite; this is already a prominent position of completeness. It is the main cranium that binds us to the inner veil of God's holy will. At the skull, session forms a closure in conversations where there may be doubt, where debate has no place, needs are met and where questions can meet answers, revelation can meet rejoicing, manifestation can meet mantles, and the anointing is accessible. The mind of God is where the word becomes approachable, and easily obtained through the cinder block of articulation that supports the auditory anointing. This communication allows one to build a parlance monument so one may speak well of God by using personal expressions, giving God all glory.

The most important point is called the Supreme Auditory Anointing. This is the jawbone that remains a movable joint, it suspends all other pathways that echo from self-glorification, that will penetrate or supersede over the chief canal that flows from one main conduit and that's the One who gives life. There is an acoustic anointing that picks up the pressure of unwanted sounds. This anointing is never hollow because it's dedicated totally to the pomegranate prayer room, where the sound only resonate the hymn of heaven. This mantra is scented with grace and bombarded with the bells of mercy. In this pomegranate prayer room is a live laboratory that is a secluded place for a prepared people, where God speaks with a resounding voice that only attracts the righteous. In this room is where worship is stored; there are no manufactured miracles, no artificial assembly. The acoustic anointing is a small sound found in the belly of the believer, this sound is not made to jointly fit with or connect with any other frequency, if tested and not proven to be balance, that sound has been illegally imitated and must immediately be sent to poison control to be disposed.

The heavenly laboratory must reject any type of strange sound that will interrupt the balance to flow throughout the body. In the acoustic anointing is the throne room of the knee, this is the most complex anatomy of the body. The knee is the crown of four major rooms: authority, perfection, completion and restoration. The knee wears special gear to cover as one goes before God. Faith completes the perfection of the joints with confidence in hope and in anticipation that God will give the victory. The tongue is a strong cartilage with authority to articulate speech in a muscular note that carries the power to command the knee to bend when the mouth speaks well of God, where the burning coals of Isaiah burns the unrighteousness so the tongue can give God glory. The favor comes from honoring God through the ligaments; God has given His approval to be flexible in His benefits, from the sacrifice of bending in devotion, bending in worshipping and bending in praising this bond of union between the blessings and prosperity that is flourished through the kneeling in submission to the Perfector. Finally there are the tissues of prayer that changes human issues into intercession by intervening ones behalf to repair the prayer junctions that left a gap between the fragrance and the aroma. The knee represents the tabernacle and the kneeling represents the altar. These two are joined at the mercy seat. The state of appearance is fastened by the presence of God, the area of the close connection is joined by the presence-chamber, and the conditions of the immediate vicinity are fused together by the present presence. The main chamber of the acoustic anointing has serum that separates the toxic temptation from the rich protein that will flow into the high place called the "heart".

Chambers of the Heart has four chambers: behind this veil you are surrounded by the power pump, that pushes continuously authority, rank, prestige, and prominent positions. The right side of the power pump receives the oil, and the left power pump, thrust the anointing through the loins, forming a layer that will cover what he has created. The four chambers release in heart rhythm and in the fullness of time to prevent from blockage. The dichotomy of the heart is the operator and the generator. The Operator locates the apex of the heart making available a complete systematic structure in the chamber. The generator provides a constant circulation back into the power pump, which permanently installs an internal circuit that includes the location, the function, the factors and the direction. These are the different ceremonious protocol that crowns the heart King. The equal alignment of the heart chamber is to crown the inner fortitude Lord of Lord. The floor plan of the heart is designed that strength with a layout in will power will give an outline that is arranged with determination. The heart can think on its own even without the mind of man, but God the chief architect has laid a firm foundation that has the perfect resume' and He hires anyone that has a whosoever will application.

The chief constituent of the heart is the backbone of dedication. This faithful bone, is structured to withstand all that comes up against the will of God. This framework is ordained to support each function that makes the heartbeat as the sound that is in heaven. The self-confidence of the circulatory ignites the power to automatically pump according to the Pentecost in the upper room, which has a sound that is never turned off. The harmony is in the key of unity with the background vocals of euphony from the heavenly host, one sound, in one place, on one accord. This must be because God does everything well and perfect for those He loves, the heavenly host only sings in the key of "A" called agreement, when this happens all under heaven must bow. All of the handiwork of God has the spine to bend and honor the utterance of the maker of heaven and earth, they are subjected to the cord in which all power and source comes from. The spine is a dichotomy with two equal structures; the top of the spine is the upper ecclesiastical where the joints stand in proxy as the preacher with the responsibility to carry the weight of the gospel and to the assembly of the upright. Then there is the lower epistle sent to send out the gospel to the weight bearer, where they will carry the letter around the belt of their belly. This is where each nerve aligns with each other, awaking each muscle and moral fiber. This gives the work experience to the upper hand of the heart. This elevated position has to support each member as an equal opportunity employer or it will not be called equilibrium. The base of the forelimb surrounds each representative; each finger has one antenna to signal every joint making sure that each function is giving the same amount of work. In order for all the members to operate equally each one is hired as the CEO of its chamber within the heart.

The pointer is for direction, the middle finger, stands in the gap for the other fingers, the ring finger is a never ending covenant between all the fingers, it promises to be remain faithful, constant and steadfast, the thumb pulls down every stronghold, and the pinkie is to diminish all flesh aroused against the knowledge of God. Without the pinkie it will only invite meandering and cause chaos in the equation.

The heart has an impressive work history, it's known for pumping the blood through the bailout drive, it forces out death through the worship of God at the same time inflates Isaiah 53:5 by inflating "but he" and enlarging "was wounded" expands "for our" and driving out "for our transgression" This assembly carries out ignorance and brings in understanding.

The right side of the heart chamber is honorable, dependable, ethical and trustworthy. While the left side is the portside of flexibility, it's adjustable to stretch pass the assignment at hand. The left side works on commission that benefits through profits and bonuses, the left side is where God sits on the throne of the heart, and the right side is where the son sits as our advocate.

Under this Chief Advocate is the supernatural heavenly house rule that is equally set up with a layout of Psalm 16:11 to distribute the word equally. The standing is the trustee board "you make known to me", the select is the council "the path of life", the special commission "in your presence there is fullness of joy;" and finally the joint that keeps the word moving is the chamber house "at your right hand are pleasures forever more." With both side equally functioning it will give a balance of:

The ability to operate (+) the flexibility to in knowing (=) riches and rewards

With this formula come solutions from the heavenly house rule, with the memo that says in Matthew 5:8 "Blessed are the pure in heart, for they shall see God." Proverbs 4:23 "keep thy heart with all diligence; for out of it are the issues of life" and Proverbs 3:5 "trust in the LORD with all thine heart; and lean not unto thine own understanding." Through these guidelines that have been approved from the anointed one with a promise of this legally binding covenant in Ezekiel 11:19, "And I will give them one heart, and I will put a new spirit within you; and I will take the stony heart out of their flesh, and will give them an heart of flesh:" The storehouse of the belly has an entrance and a exit, they are the front porch of praise and the backdoor of worship. This storehouse is situated in the midst of the absolute weightiness where it carries all the bulk in full capacity without the means of man's power.

The trichotomy of this storehouse has three levels one being the Top abdominal region which is the primary praise foundation that moves distractions to another place, for the protection of foundation. Then there is the middle or the center most dominant part that holds the weight of worship, the center of the storehouse. It holds much influence on how to rule and reign, how to take dominion and walk worthy in the Kingdom. The last part of this trichotomy is the bottom "men", a place of prayer. God lets us know that when a man prays in the bottom, his voice is called out in many dimensions. Through an " a conduit that hits three places at one time. First stop is the volume of prayer, Luke 18:1, "men ought to always pray and not faint." The second stop is the extent of prayer in James 5:16, "the prayers of the righteous availeth much" and the last place is the expansion of prayer in Matthew 17:21, "howbeit this kind goeth not out but by prayer and fasting." The seat of God's glory is in an immeasurable amount of greatness to the extent of His magnitude and richness that He so gracefully gives us daily increase of his splendor and majesty. The main conductor is this equallel-pipe driving us to the inner artery of the anointing; this canal leads the dweller to get a glimpse of God's glory as he did one of his board members Ezekiel. Inside of God's glory is an important organ called the "LIVER" this liver is not the same as one in the human body, but this liver gives everlasting life, the liver is the living. This liver met the woman at the well, he let her know that she was empty in the life that she was leading, and Jesus gave her a liver of eternal life and a well that will spring up water from eternal life. The liver was in a storage unit in room temperature glory where it held the victory for winning the war, and favor for the faithful.

This secured place is sealed and only opened when the name of Jesus is called and the blood is applied, for the blood is the source, the heritage of the saints, and the legacy from birth. In the blood is a vital component called iron. Iron in the blood cannot be moved, it's for defense, you cannot separate the bond because it's a network between agreement and confirmation, when applied it cancels debt, abandons diseases, nullifies generational curses, sends death back to the sender, and reverses all results. The liver sits on the river that refreshes the believer new every day, these rivers run parallel to the Garden of Eden. The brook of "Ingestion" is to expand, the river of Pishon. Increase the creek of "secretion" is to push out, the river of Gihon, bursting forth, the stream of "absorption" is to transfer and release, the river Tigris, rapid, the river of "excretion" is to eliminate the dead things out with a inlet of fertile fluid to push back in, the river Euphrates, source of life; fruitfulness. This blueprint helps the believer to breakthrough and survive unnecessary breakdown. These rivers of life flow from the issues of the liver's living well.

The members of this board are over a special room called the storehouse of the stomach. They sit in the boardroom of the belly, where the oracles of God are stored in the depository of the strong room. This room is designed to hold the word against the attacks of the enemy, against the fiery, fallacious darts, and most of all, against the thief who is vividly described in John 10:10. This board is set up with directors, supervisors and managers to govern the anointing. The directors oversee the patent of protection, "the thief cometh not". The supervisors are the foremen of activity in the atmosphere, "but to kill, steal and destroy" and the managers administer life back to the church when the wicked one is kept at bay, "I am come that they might have life, and they might have it more abundantly."

This vault is kept opened at all time, even during times of adversity, this depository is never depleted , or has it ever gotten down to a economical number or shape, neither does it vary by build or posture, status or rank. The storage place is a holy chamber that is never out of commission or operation. This is the belly, the strongest muscular organ in the chamber. This vital function causes power to be delegated to go in between the inner most layer of the "gloriastric" supply; this produces the greatness of God's splendor, and the majestic éclat of God. This is where the confidence of John 4:24 takes place. In this boardroom is the ark of archive where the mandate has been written in blood, the order of worship service is as follow: For the vigor of radiance, "for God is a spirit" style of approach is for "those who worship him, the élan energy is for those who "must worship him" and the dynamism activity is for those "in Spirit and truth". God has already authorized this promissory note with His intonation; His signature is the deep utterance that brings all things to current that were outstanding.

The gloriastric gland is situated in front of duo-dunamis; this organ gives the gloriastric gland two-fold units of everything. This is the leading tube that causes God's splendor to be worth the worship, His richness worth the honor, His beauty worth the prestige, and His majesty worth the praise, making His name known worth knowing him. As these board members daily gather together working as one corporation to produce a fertile harvest-time, the outgrowth from storing up the praises of God's people has he inhabits in and rest over our praise it will automatically generate a place of purpose with a communal gathering.

There is one pillar that is always on post, it is called the "shoulder". This prop withholds the foundation to the arm, the shoulder guards the entire framework of the arm, it sustains all injury and advocates all the pain so the arm will not have to feel nor become accessible to danger. The shoulder is the one that feels the infirmities of the hands, elbow and the fingers, this champion fits the description of Hebrews 4:15, "For we have not an high priest which cannot be touched with the feeling of our infirmities; but was in all points tempted like as we are, yet without sin. Yes the shoulder is symbolic of Jesus in John 19:17 "And he bearing his cross went forth into a place called the place of a skull, which is called in the Hebrew Golgotha:" the shoulder also fits the report of Isaiah 9:6 "and the government shall be upon his shoulder." The shoulders are the strongest structure that undergirds the foundation of this trichotomy, the shoulder must bear the cries of the feeble, the sleeping babies, the rest for the weary, the hugs of many that are unloved, the support of those who need healing either from death or just from loving one too much, and the betrayals of others by friendly fire. In this chamber the shoulder carries omnipresent power that has upper strength with no limitations, and no restrictions.

The roof of the shoulder is the top point that is well founded and put together not just with weakness but a hard base that is able to carry others weakness as well as the strength of its own. The shoulder stands alone because its reliable and proved to be indestructible, even through the wear and tear of others that have been abusive and have taken advantage because its built on a sturdy cornerstone. The shoulder is not like the rest of the members, because it's the bone that the body rejected and counted insignificant, it is underappreciated and regarded as one that has to do its job. The shoulder is below the shoulder value. That's why many break their shoulder sometimes in different places, because they don't know its value. For without the shoulder there is no arm, no collarbone, and no movement to assist in praise, worship or even writing.

The shoulder has a sanctuary and an altar. In the sanctuary the shoulder can rest on the things in God, for assurance and reliability, in the sanctuary it can connect to the propeller and become strengthen. The altar of the shoulder stands as advocate between the blade and the archer; it sends incense of healing back to the shoulder from wounds that have been intentionally hit. At the altar is the smoke, which a gate that connects protects and direct. At the altar is the communion connection in the upper chamber, where restoration takes place. When all this takes place, the shoulder now becomes an establishment, a ceremony, an inauguration for elevation from being just the corner to being the chief cornerstone. The shoulder now has come from a sub corporation to a "megacorp" where millions will be inducted into "upon this rock I will build my church" hall of heaven. The shoulder undergirds each part of the sanctuary within the shoulder.

In the trichotomy of the shoulder is the house of Prayer, the house of God and in the house of praise and worship. The House of God is the strongest structure built on supernumerary firebrick. The House of God is the refuge of reserve; in the house of Praise and worship is the place of dwelling in the over and beyond. The bone structure in the kingdom is now the chief cornerstone of the anatomy. In the anatomy of the house of prayer is the main muscle of invocation, which is the order that sets the tone for the timbre fragrance to be released upon His people that call upon His name. The anatomy of the House of worship is the strongest vein that carries the weight of a sincere heart and clean hands. This scent is sent back to the chamber of glory giving God back the layers of honor that are due to him. When this aligns with His will then the anatomy of the arm will build the framework that is arranged in the chamber of the upper entrance room, in this room it's called the "ark of the arm".

The order that makes this construction complete is the rotation, the extension, the pulling, the speed, and the precision. Inside the ark of the arm is the safety features that help to increase the strength for survival, it will enable the believer to experience the dichotomy of the upper strength and precision and the outer high-impact reinforcement so the believer will have authentic anointing and not prosthetic power which will only stand as a substitute, only to lead to future replacements. The main purpose for the ark of the arm is so the oil can flow freely into the different routes that it may meet back to the main system for a major supply. So when the anointing builds up, it will be conducive to the next available vessel. The anatomy of the anointing has three main arteries. The infallible intercession, this is the inner court that builds up power per second and unit of time for the sake of incapable of failing, the prescribe antidote is preserved specifically from all human errors. This perfect and precise modus operandi is used to express and not expire. The muscles of mercy are orchestrated to grant clemency by stopping the common usage the arm extends to the hand, but pushes the pressure of power that will grant greater grace to the receiver. These muscles are designed to come with a benefit package of honor, reverence and adoration. The honor is the general coverage where grace has no expiration date, and mercy is restored every time the benevolence package is still on file. Adoration is the life insurance; because the benefit law is not cheap since the glory cannot be sidestep with expensive potholes.

The honor is retroactive where there are no penalties or fees, but just compensation plus a fixed amount to spend that will be in abundance. The benefit of adoration is the 401k of faithfulness this includes greater control of the plan with favor-flow advantages there are no drawbacks, but your claim can never exceed the dedicated amount, the seraphic and cherubic protection plan covers the entire entity. These savings are for the redeemed that have not forfeited or withdrawn because of the appearance of great suffering. The Favor benefit is the pension protection plan, it has stored up approvals that are given to you at a fixed payout. The favor benefit is allocated in the anointing as an investment that is deposited in the believer with an everlasting annuity to increase the ability and benefit from the vault of heaven.

The main muscle of the ark's arm is the house of posterior power; in this house it cannot be easily broken because of the high fidelity system that protects the outer layer of the anointing, this protection encompasses loyalty that allows profit sharing. These plans are incentives that are paid straight to the ones that have fought the good fight of faith. Inside trading is priority in this plan. The trading comes directly from the encampment of secured eligibility, this host oversees the release of favor funding to the faithful, they are constantly combating and fighting on behalf of the entire called and qualified.

The divine council distributes reimbursements to the takers of the troth; those that have kept their word as a promise to the Lord of Host. In addition, they have not broken the utterance of their allegiance but have stood the test of time and gets an eternal out of pocket expense that has been summons from God, which automatically qualifies them for stock options for the obedience. It's a benefit at a fixed rate that can never be changed and never at a discount or a promotional sale. Obedience is a preplanned option with long-term compensation. Abraham's preplanned option was to give his son as a sacrifice; through obedience God gave him a long-term compensation called a "ram in the bush". This ram was Abraham's stock option at heaven's predetermined price.

This sound system secures the whole anatomy to maintain postural control, so that it may cause an automatic reflex that will respond immediately, resulting in a trifold masterpiece of quality, quantity and quantum. This triptych works in agreement to bring forth dunamis power. The arm of the ark is the apparatus to the anatomy of the leg called the lower extremity of the flute; this is the main instrument that is made of elaborate keys that causes the quality of performance to flow from the precise intonation. There are five dimensions in the anatomy of the flute; its ultimate trademark is to govern as a docent to deliver the efficient amount that is allotted to grant dominion and possess jurisdiction. There is a wind in the flute that makes a sound that warrants supremacy, this summons a trumpet that sanctifies the receiver; mandates a melodious saunter that commands the weight of God's glory to be orchestrated. This grand ensemble releases an opulence fragrance to impart order in the oil. This estate holds valuable assets called identifiers, modifiers, qualifiers, amplifiers and carriers.

Qualifiers are anatomical anointers, they are a composite of claimers that extends blood, water and power that is full of the heavenly imperial system called avoirdupois the royal metric system, a non metric system that architects that can draft the blueprint formula of arkhi+tek+ton=Chief Builder.

The Chief Builders are identifiers who establish the width of the anointing where they rule and reign in eternal to bring about into existence that is timeless and forever dwelling out of time. The anointing has an aromatic that is a permanent vapor that is irrevocable, an aromatic that is a permanent vapor that irrevocable, but it's a visible exaltation from a lofty position with extreme euphoric with exaggerated spices that comes from the power of God's presence. The Chief Builders are modifiers who are changers with height, this height cannot be removed or replaced, it sits in the throne that is being occupied by the glory, this coverage is used to reciprocate from super to supernumerary, a prescribed oil that exceeds that which is required or desired, these measurement are set in the high place and is used to canvas the distance upward indicating the altitude of the anointing.

The Chief Builders are amplifiers who increases the depth of dominion this anatomy has the power to enlarge, strength to soar and still maintaining the anointing which holds the gravity in the midst of the glory, the weight of oil is to make each measurements more in magnitude so the presence of God can rest and rule over each border and beyond reaching the righteousness of the carrier. It makes is easy to transport the anointing from side to side without the human strength, yet it's created to impregnate you with the glory of gesticulation causing a unique wave pattern that will give a high frequency of power that cannot be disturbed. The carrier is responsible to bear in the leg the power of the gospel. A carrier must not be delayed, or ahead of the scheduled time designated without being weary or bothered by the unnecessary inadequate power.

Here we have the anatomy's information center that stores a cubicle in an oubliette chamber. In this Chamber there are units with a cubicle of primary work and the shaping & installation. The Primary work is the highest rank that appoints delegates in the dichotomy system. This system consists of structure as the predominate foundation while forming and installation brings things to past. In this oubliette chamber is the highest rank called the primary work, this appoints and delegates in the dichotomy system so that the balance will consist of structure as the predominate foundation. This infrastructure has fundamental facilities that are crucial to Gods anatomy

1. "in the beginning God created the heavens and the earth

2. "In the beginning was the word"

This is the most composed anatomy in any historic publication. "In the beginning" meaning God is forever present standing identifying the one who does the qualifying. God existed before time making our time obsolete making mans theory unmatched. God has left us with the results of His anatomy in Roman 8:28 "And we know that all things work together for good to those who love God, to those who are the called according to His purpose." The installation process is to form an establishment called "head quarters" it's designed to plant your abilities in the seat of the righteous one. All data that is collected is transferred to the Engineer of Equilibrium. The anatomy of the equilibrium is the Originator, Creator and Developer, this trilogy focuses on the lateral leg of righteousness, it's the outer covering of the fibula that produces strength with a euphony effect that agrees with the weight of God's glory that will be an equivalent value and most importantly evenly proportioned towards the initial and final position.

The Originator operates the internal glory making sure that as his train fills the temple within the deep surface of God's splendor are in order with the balance of all the fibers that have banded together reflecting the left leg of his majesty and the right leg in all his greatness.

The Creator is the prime mover, God has a major paramount with an ordained order that has already been harmonious arraigned only with the classification according to a Decalogue decree, which was reserved on preorder which will before the due date of the fullness time only designated to release His greatest strength. This arrangement is called the anatomy of action, where the body cavity is cut with a small incision of influence, the spinal cord holds the condition of the nerve in order to discern the function of wisdom while the cortex builds the outer layer of understanding with explicit instructions on this set up protocol. The Developer is an anointed agent who is the host that supports specifically towards the shape and balance of the autonomy bone. This bone is liberated from any external valve that needs a device in order to function. The developer initiates a pivotal point; it increases the capacity as it expands to full range. This anointed agent sits in the orchestrated desk of a developer, arranging in triad the consistency of a photosynthesis producer who is a respiration administrator who prepares the harvest by planting seeds of soil solution which is called domain infusion where two mixtures that has collided together to cause a balance to the author of autotrophic, this anointing requires high honor as nutrition and adoration in the vitamins as the main source.

The anatomy of the power flex: this allows the main faculties to generate constant movements. These active applications are paired and synced to the chamber that is located in the center of the circulatory muscle, this muscle helps to move the power weight back and forth keeping a balance for the mere fact of "let God arise, let his enemies be scattered" This muscle is contracted to transport the blood back into the powernary lifeline. This chamberlatory section is responsible for connecting the eternal posterior and the lateral of the leg. This process is to supply a permanent refuge that will be conducive to take dominion. The significance of this mass movement is that all internal and external abilities become unified in hegemony. Hegemony is the framework that supports the external fabric of supremacy, which is highly compatible to his beauty and honor making his sovereignty stand in agreement with the internal greatness.

The anatomy of dominion specializes in extensions that are meant to go beyond the normal limits, this anatomy exaggerates God who is the prime mover of all that is internal establishes imperial rule over all the primary vitals that balance the body functions. This royal upper class noblesse is an endless resource of life sustaining that is indispensable organs which is the heart that carries the beat through to prevent backflow, the arteries carries away unwanted agents to blend in and take away the content that supplies important routes to righteousness. The inner layer of the arteries is lined with a cover to conceal the sin that was veiled by the cross with an endless supply of blood that brings nutrients from the altar, order to confirm and life everlasting. The vein is the chariot that transport huge tubes of vital fluids, there are reliable deposits of oil with critical content that involves rapid power and plasma . The dominion flex takes up resident to protect, preserve and provide a foundation for the internal rotation a supernatural line that connects two dimensional structures: the horizontal vibrations and the vertical voice. The vertical voice speaks in a bolted upright position that is directly towards each angle for the purpose of alignment. The horizontal vibrations are parallel associates that have equivalent perpendicular power for the main purpose that every angle has the balance of the anointing that it may serve and be evenly distributed. So each surface can maintain the position of authority. The anatomy of the authority flex is the primary place of accommodations. The major anatomy of the authority is the circulatory command, which rotates to keep the rules generated by the Ruler. The respiratory charge is the demand to make a consistent ventilation and muscular sovereignty, which is an active movement with supreme rights to maintain posture. Dominion triplicates a three-fold stream that is always in a current well built fibrous freight, this means of outlet is always a tenacious presidium. The Sovereignty summons a decree to mandate establishment. Dominion gives free endorsements to expand jurisdiction that will empower, maintain and uphold the position of authority.

THE BLOOD BANK OF THE ANOINTING

This chamber is where the constant flow of cells from the righteous, this compartment has a cavity where there is unlimited watercourse through a tube that will allow clear conduit to enter and exit. This bank accumulates mass amounts into the vault where there is unlimited accommodation for the blood. This bank is reservoir with large amounts of resources where one can come as a safe haven in the doors of the sanctuary and find peace in the holy place. The blood is an exchequer to reserve for rewards of the righteous, where they can obtain mercy in the presence of God. The blood bank of the anointing is a depot that holds immeasurable supply that spring forth from the mercy seat as the glory of God saturates the reservoir. In this blood bank there are vaults where the savings deposit are kept, each vault holds unlimited amount that has been accrued since the time of redemption.

Blood is delivered new every morning through an armored chariot that carries a decree for the redeemed as a reminder that we can go boldly to the throne of Grace and obtain mercy through this conduit Isaiah 53:5 But he was wounded for our transgressions, he was bruised for our iniquities: the chastisement of our peace was upon him; and with his stripes we are healed." this transportation chariot brings large quantities of answered prayers from the saints, healing for the nation, safety for the leaders supernatural miracles signs and wonders, sickness and diseases, the family, jobs and homes. This is from the prayers of the righteous to fill into every account that sits at the altar ready to be filled and manifested. Because of the numerous amounts of prayers for coverage the Blood Bank of the Anointing has a balance sheet with a triad anointing. The three set the tone for even distribution: Access, Eternity, and Commission. The Access allows the redeemer to collect heavens currency even when the earth is in famine, deficit and money seems to be scarce, the redeemer can always withdrawal from the faith account and be rewarded.

The redeemer doesn't have to worry about expiration dates on their membership card because eternity is without numerical end, so the redeemer can go to the equity counter and draw from the well that will not run dry, this account is for valued vessels that have not abused transaction for selfish ambition, but have used the principle of "seek ye first" And finally the redeemer can reap from the commissions capital, where shareholders can withdrawal from the favor fund, faith investment, praise contribution and retained earnings from their worship. The anatomy of the access account is security through sanctification, increased prepaid expenses, and fixed levels of income that is released from a trust fund that is secured in through heavens estates.

The Anatomy of Heavens estate: empyrean, paradisiacal, firmament, kingdom, and the throne of God. The "empyrean" is the eyes of upper echelon where many can look to the hill from which cometh their help, it's where the righteous can run in and be safe, the empyrean is a wonderful fitting to abide under the shadow of the Almighty. The paradisiacal is the mind, where the righteous can rest and the glory of the Lord will overshadow and anything dead has to be resurrected. The firmament is the feet where God expanse your territory guiding you to a source that is arranged to help you get results in your time of need, The LORD God is my strength, and he will make my feet like hinds' feet, and he will make me to walk upon mine high places -Habakkuk 3:19.

Finally the kingdom which is your body, your body is the temple of the Lords because He is the ruler with a position that represents and independent position that needs not to apply for an application for a hierarchy with a time that is endless and forever. The kingship is the main branch that displays the hierarchy order from empire to estate; they are equally measured to accommodate the uniformity of esteem, honor and admiration. The dimension of this radius is an uninterrupted continuance only increasing the dynastic birthright. There is a genetic formula to this kingship: vital fluid, legacy physique and intense vigor. The authority of the kingship is the position by the Chief presidium, which possesses the region of royalty that has the entrepreneur of strength, and power of tenacity. The triplicate of this great inheritance is the monarch that is the sole and absolute ruler, the prime arch that oversees the Spinal support of the body; this ruler will also endorse a triad that is of rank, estate and order. The formal rank is extracted from the life of the blood which ignites the caliber of his character. The classical rank is the soul, the nucleolus which is the center of endurance, the intestinal will power and the belly is the loins of the birth right which allows him to see the manifestation. Finally the order of the seraph Spine, which is the base of the back so that the column of display will be the fiber that is cut with approval of authority, weight and richness, with the power and the seal of qualification makes this Blood bank of Anointing effective. In the Early American melody by William Cowper "There is a fountain filled with blood, Drawn from Immanuel's veins;" This Bank is a spiritual wellspring made available to all that want to be cleansed, washed and purged with hyssop. This bank never needs an overnight deposit because it's a guarantee bloodline with a warranty in birthright, and surety of kinship.

THE FEET OF THE FIRMAMENT

The Anatomy of God's feet, the balance and the equality on which He stands. These are the functions that are in place to cause Heavens to be his throne and the earth is foot stool. The bones, joints and muscles allow God to be ruler over all, stand in the midst of the storm and defeat the enemies of God. The feet of God has no division but are carefully clothed in the depths of his resplendence. God displays his radiant majesty through the firmament of his forefoot. All the richness sits in the upright position of support his balance and mobility. These three works in whole high ranking they are equivalent to the heavens numerical name called "GRACE"

The feet of God are solid, rigid and unyielding, His feet is firmly placed in the royal living quarters in the upper echelon. The first anatomy is the Junction Joints, they are the bonding of all activities together, signaling the heart of the feet that will cause communion with the sole of the feet where the base and balance becomes one, by connecting the foundation of the arch which is to build a bridge to connect the mighty and strong ligaments together so that they may provide a structure throughout the body of the feet. The feet has ears to hear what the Spirit says to the body, how to react and get in alignment with what is going to happen in the earth. This will bring flexibility to the trichotomy network. This circuitry is called the connecting of the joints; this is designed to bring union between the fiber of favor and the footlet of faith together. The footlet is the vein to the gospel "How beautiful upon the mountains are the feet of him that bringeth good tidings" Isaiah 52:15. The fiber is strategically woven and cut so divinely with humans' hands so that every strand can meet the requirements of equilibrium. This brings on the acoustic sound of heavens doxology that allows our feet to go into overdrive not overdraft where it will be lacking the power to stand. Inside of the feet is a chamber that sends an offertory melody that makes the saints rejoice and Satan to run. The feet of God is to defend for the Saints at all cost, in the defending is the columns of victory, they are attached to each of the fibers that connect to the muscles of righteousness and uprightness, this will cause a great movement among the soul of the feet hardening the feet to stand, and having done all to stand, STAND!

In the anatomy of the standing is the threadwork of loyalty, the commitment that has the trimmings of faith, the ornaments of order, that is cradle in a caudex crib that is secured with the gates of trust, order and surety, these gates is trimmed with an appliqué embroidery that is crossed stitched with the finest brocade of dependency. God's feet is laced with the finest of all, that's what's makes him governor of the nations. In this legislative body is an important shield called "BONE THE BUILDER" has a trichotomy of "The Plan of Protection" "Design for the muscle mobility" and "Created for interior strength" This is the committee that has been set up for the front line of the past, present and future. This anatomy is responsible for assembling, increasing and strengthening. The anatomy of the assembling is that the builder has put in a place a "Plan of Protection", there is a form inside that is strategically and systematically fashioned to the foot to be an original archetype. In this plan of protection and security action plan is instituted. This security plan is the seal that guards every step that is cut perfectly to the heel, so that the heel can appoint support and put a motion plan to the foot. The heel conducts a written a hymn that only the structure of the foot can understand. The foot assembles an orchestra and the instep is the chorus line while the toes keeps the beat, they all together makes a sound either of war or of victory.

This heavenly arrangement is to agitate the adversary for the purpose of rerouting the dispensation of danger. In this chaotic affair between danger and demise the feet is to send a signal to all the assembly that there is an appointment to defeat death at all cost. God who is the prime mover who is the author and finisher of our faith, God who is the inventor, He is the master builder; he is the preeminent planner, the stimulator, motivator and the originator. God who is the chief specialist has provided us with the plan of protection, he also instituted specific degrees of muscle mobility, this specialist has now given us freely the mobile adapter that will connect us with the best, making it suitable for all battles, so that we can withstand, confront and resist. God has designed the balance of the feet to make adjustability flexible, so the inside of the foot chamber will scan out a prescription that is constantly written for the intensity of endurance, this prescription will provide ferocity, force and fanaticism that will ignite extreme zeal towards greatness. In the foot chamber the feet has its own pharmaceutical its already manufactured and approved to provide medicine towards all that are a threat to the saints of God. In this chamber no genetic, nothing but genuine is produce for the sake to cure, treat, and prevent death and diseases.

The diagnosis has already been preplanned so the feet releases a formula that will alert the tissues of this special order so the right amount of dose can be given. When the bones releases a demand the muscles then collaborate with the membrane of the music transmitting the sound of broadcast to the bones so the mobility of the feet can move freely not on a count as horses but on command as the army of the Lord. The blue print establishes a canticle anthem, for the feet this psalm is a coded called HALLELUJAH! It is arranged only in foot format in the key of heaven. The foot format is of high honor, so much that praise has to be escorted by a dance that will cause a revival in the ligaments of the leg, when that happens the stirring up of the bones like in Ezekiel will become like of flesh, and when they become of flesh then they create an interior strength to the soul of the feet the center and focal point of power. The mainstream midline sets the midfoot in locomotion once the arch has been lifted then freedom starts within and without, making the foot lightly in battle and to walk heavy in the gospel that's where the heel and the hind foot meets. The structure of the foot bears the weight of worship. The foot is the finish line of triumph, you cannot run, leap, or even stand strong in the days of adversity if your foot has no interior strength. The formal style of the feet is created to give power; so much it has its own zip code, where it is only registered in the house of the Lord because of the high volume supply of strength the number is unlimited yet perfect. The force and capacity will equal the power.

ABOUT THE AUTHOR

Reared in a home polished by the beauty of Christian principles, Pastor James A. Crawley, and Evangelist Dora L. Crawley cultivated the formative years of their daughter, Anita, with the academic, spiritual and social substance to make a difference through her service to humanity. Anita, a full-blooded offspring of the Church of God in Christ was singled-out with cognitive promise at an early age, explaining her uninterrupted academic succession from Newark Public School System through Essex County College with a concentration in Business Administration. Anita has also been awarded an honorary doctorate of divinity from the Grace Theological Seminary.

Summarily, two significant callings comfortably rest upon her with honor and conviction.

First, the call to share the Gospel. Her preparation for this adventure was achieved at Screven Memorial Bible Institute in Newark, New Jersey while concurrently serving in the public sector through New Jersey Transit's Contract Compliance Division. Her second calling is recognized and practiced in the honorable role of "cleaving to her husband" and ministering the transfer of her upbringing to the children she and her husband, Michael, share: Nicole, Brian, and Joshua. Her full-time career as a "stay at home mom" is one from which she draws down benefits of immeasurable fulfillment.

Anita is an active, capable and energetic woman of diverse accomplishments, suited for typifying the balance of dedication to her home, service to her church and outreach to mankind.

Anita asserts, "The ultimate goal of my ministry is to impact a nation that will drive a surge of influence where people of power can become the lens that mirrors the image of God."

Anita is the founder and president of A Snowden ministry, Inc. Anita and Michael, whose marriage covenant thrives upon the agreement that "God is a good God even on a bad day," make their home in Hinesville, Georgia.

To Contact of For Booking Information:
A Snowden Ministry, Inc.
Hinesville, GA
912.335.4434
Email: asnowden.ministry@yahoo.com